THE HONEY

DIVYA VORUGANTI

WORKBOOK PRESS LLC
187 E Warm Springs Rd,
Suite B285, Las Vegas, NV 89119, USA

Website:	https://workbookpress.com/
Hotline:	1-888-818-4856
Email:	admin@workbookpress.com

Ordering Information:
Quantity sales. Special discounts are available on quantity purchases by corporations, associations, and others.
For details, contact the publisher at the address above.

ISBN-13:   978-1-957618-87-6 (Paperback Version)

REV. DATE: 22/07/2022

Preface

My name is Divya Voruganti Sabarwal. I am a very simple woman when it comes to friendship and loyalty. This book is dedicated to my family and friends. The biggest feature of my book is that I am on a particular subject, but what I have learned from my life has not come to my mind. I kept writing with whatever I thought from the heart because I used to think that yes, what I needed in my life I could have what I need in everyone and in life. I can hear the words and understand what is in my life. You may have problems listening to them, but when you understand this book, you will also realize that yes, the specialty of this book is that it is not written for anyone, especially on the year, which was felt on the heart. I know very well you are more intelligent and reconciled than me, but I still tried in such a way for people understand me.

I was almost lost from life, but then I realized how many people are like me, who spoiled their lives by being upset about such trivial matters, so I thought I would give people hope. I will give it a very good shot, possibly the best shot I can try. I am thinking that hearing my words can solve the problems of my life, and the biggest thing that I am sharing with you is that my dream in life is to write a book and become a writer. Hope you enjoy this book full of quotations on my real experiences. Enjoy.

At the end, I would like to thank my husband for encouraging me to write and prompt my write-ups. And to the spirit of my father, whom I call Papa, that guided me in the dark, thank you. My heart is full of gratitude for every encouragement I get to write.

Introduction

I like to listen to people's beliefs, and it forms a strong impact on the social and economic patterns. I believe we need relationships to connect and cogitation to be triumphant.

As a child, I promised my father that I will paint the world and I will make it a better place. As a child, I loved colors, shades, and tints. I usually give my art therapy through my quotations on Facebook as I feel an artist can paint through the mind all the colors and patterns. I can see colors and patterns in people, and I explored all this through music and lyrics with number patterns and lines.

I wish to start an organization, which I decided on in 2016. I had been working on it. It's for people to find their purpose in life and know about their own higher self and move to the path of self-realization. I imagined it in my dreams and in reality. It's a beautiful thought, and it can lead humanity to a very new, balanced equation.

I wish to form a connection, a bridge between art and science, and I feel it's a global affair. I can feel the pitch low, medium, and high. I feel you are more fulfilled the happier you feel, and fulfillment is very authentic and unique to each individual. I wish to set an example of fulfillment, and my fulfillment is in colors, patterns, numbers, music, and my family. I wish to make the world a better place to live in for my very own family. I value family first.

I would like to pursue a community service group with a concept. My philosophy is that you must love your power and know yourself. I would like to help people be connected with the community. My emphasis is on body-and-mind training through different mediums of art, which is called Kala. Art is not only accomplished with a paintbrush, pencil, or ink; for some, art is found in dance, music, cooking, sports, and budgeting. There are various mediums of art. Art, the Kala, and the science of art, the Vigyan, are designed to train your mind to be fit, to find a way to live comfortably.

My concept is simple: to help you obtain a peaceful, healthy mind-and-body experience. The Kala is the skill that is used to create a pattern of well-being for every person. I believe a supportive community with mentors all around the world can give the key to working on a healthier you, both in mind and in body.

My methods are simple: I help you cope with social, familial, and environmental pressures. I would like to do this with training provided by skilled professionals (the masters of KalaVigyan) who are available to the public. All these professionals are available to work with you online. They will work through the various mediums of art and help everyone prepare for a better today and a great future. Each professional is prepared to provide you guidance about awareness and to help you find a path to follow to achieve goodness.

We know that mindfulness and awareness sometimes require education. Not everyone understands how to achieve their potential. We can help you unleash these powers and, in doing so, teach you how to excel in every area of your life. Each one of the methods we teach is designed by teachers. They have unique experiences to help you learn how to cope, reduce stress, and live a more satisfying life.

Every day is a new beginning. Every day is a new day.

Becoming nothing is just giving away baseless characteristics that are harmful to yourself and others.

Destiny and luck only glow if we use our minds right in good care for one another.

If God gave us the mind to think, make use of it well enough so we won't be trapped in a baseless destiny and luck game.

Destiny and luck, everything incorrect can change your circumstances with a little effort, doing so happily from social and environmental pressures.

Grace God great granted gratitude.

I claim to be happy as it's the best pain full of pleasures. I am happy doing my homework and classwork well.

Karma Yogi, a healer, can read details.

To be a Buddha is not easy, but to adapt him into your soul is OK, because my love is Buddha, the infinite mind.

Add wanted + delete unwanted – subtract dead. Divide yourself to cherish to multiply.

When we are sad or exploited for our own peace, let that shit go for good.

Live life with fun. Find direction that you like and fly. Just don't bother of creepy monsters who discourage you, but for yourself, see all the negatives and positives.

Listen to your perfect mind in frame.

Make a strong prayer. It will go far in the universe then reflect back if intentions of good prosperity increases. Prayers can solve the mystery of known and unknown intentions.

Maybe it's a race, a super creature race of all social animals, every day without a notice of marathon.

Where there is insecurity, it's hell. Get out. Jump out. There is no calm, no love, no patience.

People get crazy over love and love no more for real. They just have selfish intentions. So if you don't know how to love, learn to care.

The thing that put smiles on faces are hot sellers! Soul takes nothing but experiences.

Yoga teaches openness of the mind and flexibility that's infinite.

Controlling turbulence is to set free the chains. Set free others and yourself.

Connections hold no distance, but barriers do.

Story of Transformation

White, the color of purity, is given to the black snakes and purple lizards. It's a transformation of souls. There is a sacrifice. Elton John is right— hearts live in separate worlds. It's no sacrifice, yet there is a sacrifice of the color bend. In dreams, black and purple become white, with purple stripes on a lizard. Just like a tiger, the bend changed. To stripes like tiger— it's a saying, a Chinese saying. I don't know for white snakes and lizards becoming white, but purple is a deep transformation of the soul and the x generation forever and ever. Connections are destined to happen to change the fate. I wish prosperity to them forever and ever, for all the new lives. Yes, I am a thief. I stole the identity of the snakes and lizards to purify the universe. I did it. It's my karma. I can't help it. But I never think in duality; I only think to be one in duality. No dark matter can unbind the oneness ever. It's stranger than fiction in reality, as strange to you as it is to me. I cry☹; hence, it's the truth. The deepest secrets want to let it go in the block chain of connections. The color white is pure and beautiful. It's shiv; it's the path to shiv and the everlasting power, the Brahma, the truth in the ultimate reality.

It's not only charity, but everything

Begins at home

In duality, we exist only if we let go of the darkness. Night shall pass to the brightest days. Forget about winning or losing; just play. Discontentment rises when hoping too high. Have a sportsmanlike spirit. Never ever give up your show. Be a player.

Music gives happiness. Before I can create, I listen patiently to all the sounds around me carefully, both the high pitch and the low. I understand all of them, knowing I can feel.

God gives power

To courageously face people with arrogance, lies, and cheats. I don't go against them knowingly; I can just ignore them.

A generous person will be humble and kind always, doesn't matter

Whatever it takes

So power, if money is not the reason of arrogance, it's the character of the person.

Yes, power shows the true character faster.

Generosity remains the same, and so does arrogance. Power is fire and increases both persons yet the same, either generous or arrogant.

Levels of high grades or low don't matter to test a character.

Yes, when high powered at a low pitch can analyze better.

I am what I want to be

8 + 9 = 17, 8 + 9 = 1 + 7 = 8

8 being infinity

Yin/yang

I believe in the power of colors, lines, and numbers

Matter that's friendly

Integrity, faith, trust at stake

*Solitude, the medicine; or get integrity, faith, trust back with returns
and interest*

Do nothing

Insect is the ant. It works hard in togetherness.

The ant is the master of time chain.

*You— the manager, only the manager— don't work, only excel— no
XL.*

Get out of the trap of only being a manager. Be a laborer to know.

Either have the meat or die

Death is suicidal

Either have the luxuries or misfortune

Choose freedom

Thoughts have no license, no state identifications, no certifications. It's liberal of liberty.

Yes, it's okay to forgive and forget, but asking for forgiveness and forgetting the actions you did by erasing them can only become real in the present and future if you pray to be forgiven. Yes, we sometimes consciously or unintentionally unconsciously hurt. We need to ask for forgiveness before forgiving and forgetting because sometimes forgiving and forgetting becomes hard. We can't forget even if we forgive to get rid of all these chains. In time, we should pray with our own true hearts for forgiveness to the divine. There is someone who is going to answer our prayers. Believe me, there will be someone out there looking to approach or answer our prayers. Keep your intentions clear and clean.

Yes, it's okay to let people know you're hurt 😢, it's okay to express it, and it's okay to have hard feelings sometimes; but it's always straight and right to ask for forgiveness in prayers because it's their karma what they do and it's all yours what you intend to do. Bad thoughts come; they shall make you restless, impatient. Maybe you do certain actions that you don't intend to do to stay away from those thoughts. It's good to pray to the divine power every day. You may think it doesn't even exist. You have thoughts like "It's only me," but something within us—even if we are all different, individualistic people—keeps us connected in a blockchain.

We are all connected. We want that connection. We dwell and are eager for that supreme connection with our collective body and mind. We connect with some people we can connect and others we can't connect. It's the yoga rule" we all connect to those individuals of the same category, like the caterpillar, and we are butterflies. We live in the lotus effect in the world to become perfect, as the lotus pond is a pond of divine connection taken to the supreme of you.

Study the lotus pond. Everything that goes into the pond changes its nature and characteristics. Creatures live long in the lotus pond, and they change. The changes that happen in the pond are that some become weak and some become strong, and it's in the muddy, stagnant waters that the lotus grows. The lotus flower is a symbol of perfection. It blooms for a very short time. The moon, the air, the rain—all the natural factors play a very important role in the lotus effect. It's a beautiful example of perfection— the happiness, the truth and the love. ♡

Tug-of-wars

Stepping up or pulling up good, may it be anyone. If it's hard to pull up, do it in togetherness

Respect

Do before you ask

Don't launder; be harmonious

Communities should understand the basic needs and match the purpose of people in life, not fight against nature.

It's not modern thinking or traditional, old-school thoughts if you cut pace with the environment's basic needs.

Promote people to work, not beg. It's how you design the environment we live in that matters.

Money is important to everyone!

Not supporting beggary is understandable.

But not giving them knowledge and work is not x getting in my head.

Don't support anyone who sheds crocodile tears.

The jug is full of water. Being a sage, I don't have the thirst.

It's my destiny, my luck.

Maybe that jug of water is used as a big portion of ocean to spread real happiness and harmony.

Transformations happen.

I dream of transformation; it gives me tears. I feel the pull of attachments being detached.

Dreams are very powerful resources

In dreams, we imagine

Imagination is the master of inventions and discoveries

Destiny depends on karma, actions, or

Thoughts ⚬. It feeds on them

Your body and mind depend on it

Keep intentions straight.

Erasing, changing, deleting x memory can change our present and future forever and ever.

Is it possible?

Don't think like a wavering mind.

Life goes with flow; no barriers. Rain lets the clouds pass.

Don't do if than else.

I can be your hero!

You laugh; I laugh.

If you cry, I am here to help.

Let that shit go.

Always look at the bright side of everything; never lose hope.

Love can change everything around—

Truth, faith, and trust!

We desire in love.

In love, we acknowledge, we accomplish, we understand, we secure, we change!

It's perfection.

Is life just a TED Talk? Or

More experience of practicality to it?

It's always the act and speech of kindness that can make the tables turn.

Kindness is not an illusion; it's pure and cleanses the soul.

Three sweet Ps:

Prosperity

Perseverance

Peace

In the mirror, I see the real me, my reality, not limited to beauty. It's beyond. Look deep within the mirror.

The beast always wins over beauty

Because in reality, the beast is inside us. The real me, the perfect me—it gives me a reality check.

Shared work

Shared experience

Is also sharing and caring

It's not limited to material things.

Actions speak always louder than words.

Where there is love, there's liberation in thoughts and actions.

Freedom exists.

I reflect, and my reflections are cast on the matter I like.

Retaliate

To

Compression, merge in union, then scatter in frustration.

For me, beauty is in being neutral and originally ordinary.

Emotions

We love to love, not to hate + + = +.

Love is infinite.

What goes with your soul is engraved on the mind.

Time is limited

Depends on relativity.

Love is unlimited

Depends on emotions and care.

Pay back

With smiles.

Be against

Violence,

And never provoke violence.

I strongly

Agree that machines and AI can help us against

Physical and mental tortures! They are of great help stepping up and pulling up.

People who mentally torture is predictable, a safeguard feature.

You can think two steps ahead of those people.

Physical torture, you still forget that's the power of mind over matter.

Mental tortures go with your soul.

Everyday we refine

$$$$$OR

Re-re-refined

Ourselves.

The biggest independence

Makes your happiness.

Free

Put smiles and keep smiling.

Prayers make a difference even if we see God as an imaginary power. It's the prayers and devotion.

The universe works together with me, for me, by me. Every dark night shall pass. I will stand out. I will never give up my emotional intelligence.

New way, laugh and increase laughter

Live and let live, as if we were on a battlefield

Cry and make cries sadist

What you like

Circle ◯, circle ◯, then in a loop of infinity

Keep going round and round about for happiness

It looks like we walk in straight lines. Actually we circle, circle.

Just be happy 😆 😁 😄 😃, no reasons required

Five stars ★★★★☆

Declaration

No riches, no apologies, no thanks. Just be one with yourself

With who you are.

Criteria 1

Be thankful, have gratitude than happiness, than rich, no if no; but

Only a loop of than, than

Happy

Honestly

I lived in solitude for the past twenty years, and I am still living n it.

Need to press the Home button.

It's always better to pop up, put appearance in, and put thinking in perspective then pop like a fizzy ball.

The third eye hesitancy

The body and soul need different items on the to-do list

Constant scramble

Really

Hot or cold

Only my destination is spirituality

I read, write, and learn details; that's my way to meditate on my higher self to boost myself and serve as a product of prosperity shared diligently.

Great philosophies come from heartlands of golden birds. From my heart, the philosophies served in the prosperity is far better than welfare allowances because prosperity leads to care first and then serve others as much as you can limitlessly.

Buddha said, "*Suffering is caused by desire.*" But we like to suffer. There is no end to sufferings as our bodies are made to take sufferings. The choice is ours. We take suffering with pain, pleasure, or perseverance.

It's not the game of likes.

It's all coming together on the same platform, creating machines, following each other's patterns, which are more productive. No one is 100 percent.

If I am happy I am alive,

Then

I am rich!

1 Life

Be one 👆 .

Integrity in diversity can be united.

You follow your own path straight; keep up with your own powers.

Awareness exists; make a difference. You should not be affected.

Imagination

Knowledge

Wisdom

Motivation

Come in all the dreams

Don't have any knowledge; have common sense.

The basic instinct comes first!

Out-of-the-box theory is true

Knowledge is created outside.

Will always do what my heart ♡ tells me to.

It will always have voices, and make you smiled at your judgment on willpower.

Don't crave for more than what is required. Don't' crave on buying or spending earning; just crave on pulling yourself and others up.

To meditate, you don't need to go anywhere, nowhere. Just be present. Just be, not even within, but you need to work out and master your own skills!

First, get out of your mind's clever traps; first, learn to forgive yourself and then others!

Om Mangalayam

Forgiveness = human

It is not a question of being god or demon.

It's a question of being divine; positivity leads to initiative.

All you need is yourself.

If you lose yourself, then everything is gone! Don't lose your real self.

Strange, very strange I may be! If I hold the infinite calculations, be finite. I did it at repeat mode with logic and creativity only.

Who loves to work out

Is the master of inspiration!

Work is service; it's not labor of hard and smart. It's unconditional, not for attraction, not for grant, but for helping one another!

Left brain / right brain

Thinking coordination and balance with exercise on any topic at repeat mode

Work is true meditation!

Design thinking can only be mastered if we know the lines and the complexity and simplicity of the lines.

Do everything with a true heart.

Keep your calculations and screen neat and clean inside and outside.

Unaware factor may be very strong, but if you aren't courteous, it exists. Else awareness doesn't just keep up your good work.

Keep mind in clarity

For self!

Your mind will reflect in the actions of others!

Explain yourself.

Never give up loving what inspires you.

Only give up

Ignorance and arrogance

Strong persons never give up, never run away!

A failed person has a better understanding toward what is missing out; it's a learning experience for the next levels of performance.

Rigidness shows only to perform duties. That's unconditional care. Love like donating for real in service.

Ignorance or arrogance, yes, it's very true. In my experience, women become enemies of one another faster.

Not all though! It shouldn't be.

Globe 🌍

Or universe—locations keep changing: A can be B or B or be C or C can be A. You never know! Predictions can.

Cheats here and there.

But the formula of possibilities is always good to use in life. Neglect unimportant stuff, prioritizing need.

A new story in the market shakes the stock numbers' machines with history of stories, as stories repeat itself. Retrieve faster.

To pin down someone, you calculate accurately what that person likes, wants.

Just do it with new balance.

Nothing's impossible.

Great cooking

Is a fine art with

Keeping the flavor of basic

Beastly elements and science in mind and then working on the beauty of details.

Ravishing knowledge

The divine power

Gateways to wisdom

No to ignorance and delays in performing daily chores or rituals.

Be strong enough and prepared enough, just like building a structure. Even if you break it, it can automatically be rebuild. Don't break.

The beauty of the source is one, two, three.

But we are all made of different components, as we don't act on the same levels.

Our bloodstream differs.

Karma yogi

Do whatever is needed in the time flow and keep intentions clear and don't rely for fruit.

It will be served in time

Arrogant people only like you because you can be a ladder to success or they can dig gold from you.

They don't understand the meaning of friendship.

You are a fool if you think you can change arrogant people and teach them to be humble.

They deserve to be pushed by the world.

Boycott

Arrogant people; don't let them

Suck your blood.

People who make your life beautiful, be with them, not the ones who constantly complain because they will suck you.

I am not only bold or beautiful but also dedicated and not a cheater, liar, or hypocrite.

As a woman, I am getting tired.

Spreading pollution is damn simple, but clearing it out from

Within

Goes in the tube of time.

You can never have a good, stable force of manpower, a land of happiness until you set tags to each power righteously.

We play only one game. It's known as eco monopoly, but no revolution spreading pollution.

On our planet Earth, everything has a price tag. Aren't we getting bored with these price tags?

I don't know if you agree with this statement. There are no free lunches!

Where there is insecurity, there is no

Love, so get out of that hell.

Stop giving shoulders to people to cry on because it's worthless, as they will break your shoulders.

I have a dream that we all should have beautiful hearts ♡ and

Minds aligned together.

Don't do the same mistake on a repeat mode.

Encourage one another; we are not animals.

We are social.

Everyone should have a brave heart to admit their faults no matter how ugly they are.

Don't cry. Just admit and carry on.

On

Lever that I will create flowers will not lose their entities.

Is not a question of men or women.

It's the weak entity.

For my own peace and harmony, I choose

To forgive people

And carry on with life

Shanti, shanti, om

I love the green!

My green planet!

The only thing I like is if you put a smile on faces! From this earth, the soul takes nothing but experiences.

We all can't do only one thing. We are all made to do different, different jobs; else, the world will never work. We depend on one another.

Why beg work for your living? Why still earn for your living? Why cheat on the love of your life?

Both my hands come together to Allah for

11.11

In my child's pose.

Sportsmanlike spirit should be in every individual. You should not end up until you hit the target. Never give up if it's for good.

Everyone deserves

Respect. 🛡 Don't let bad feelings overtake you.

Learn to love and educate people and give them keys to open doors of success!

Socially never exploit

Innocence.

Our flowers should be raised without abuse!

Open the mind

Infinity

That's what yoga teaches.

Hindu hai

Hum vatan hai

Ye Gulsitan Hamara Hamara

We are Bhartiya.

But with all diversities of religions and cultures,

We are called Hindu.

Every day is another day! Make it bright. Paint good colors.

Never feel

You are chained.

Free yourself and free others; that's the formula to control turbulence!

Our world is ugly, and that's the beauty of it.

Make no judgments; just keep up the good work.

Acceptance is divine.

Care is holy.

Men are good at their work.

Women are good at their jobs.

And as a collaboration, they are great. Be friends.

Perfect balance is a child in the middle of Daddy and Mommy walking together.

Not Daddy taking all the stress.

I am very happy in virtual reality if I can

Listen 👂 to anyone and give solutions.

But to myself, am I ready yet?

People talk nonsense over and over. I reveal the identity, and not get 👂

To me, it looks like I have come out of my cave!

Connections hold no distances, but barriers do!

Go for real, not duplicate, not artificial.

Give me satisfaction.

I am not here to pay your price.

Feed their egos, give them

Satisfaction, whatever it takes, but don't fight them.

Protect your home. I am not playing no middle monkey and no shared cat.

No one plays me; I'll set an example for you.

Do fear them.

They'll destroy you, but if you marry, keep satisfying their ego.

Can't cover up the hollow

My shoes lost

My Hermès lost

My cash flow going reverse!

Feel very guilty

No sorry

I can't apologize

No apologies; I just earned disrespect

If you make more songs, more stories.

Imperfect I need time.

I feel if my integrity and faith are questioned, I should just start new beginnings!

Time

In space to relax, play, enjoy.

No prize, just price.

As women, we stand for one another. If they can be sluts, we can be sluts, but you can't demoralize and be real. Never let a sword come out.

We as humans have the power to create.

However, we aren't animals or machines.

When we race, we are.

Here I am to take you by the hand on the road that leads to happiness and success to fulfill your dreams. Am I a guide or a fool?

In duality, we exist only if we let go of the darkness. Night shall pass to the brightest days. Forget about winning or losing; just play.

You tell me to be open-minded. I am open-minded, but I can't shut down on your ship and take disgrace for cleaning your dirt!

Fortunate is the one who knows it rains when a storm comes, leaving egos behind. It's okay to be flexible.

The five elements are the connection of the heart to the mind when it knows its powers right. What I am doing is absolutely right.

Even if you all the terminology and languages but if you don't have a consciousness gift 💝, can you treat? No, you need to use your hands and mind. Dirty them, and lose your heart. No stealing, cheating, telling lies to yourself or chasing others. Be your own beast; that's the beauty to protect, to save. Shakespeare said it all right: nothing lies in the name. It's in the patterns; It's your fingerprints making. Yes, indeed, it is. You have to break the chain. Maybe you are cursed. Always say "Please let me be a better version only of my own self," and the gates will open to you because maybe it's not you but the deeds of your forefathers. It's okay. Don't use or feed on ego. Chase it; cast it. Just do you because it's only you who can your own purpose; otherwise, action replays.

The Scientific Perspective of Meditation

From a scientific perspective, how does meditating affect your body? During meditation, we can see an increase in brain regions directly correlated with decreased anxiety and depression, along with more tolerance for pain. The default mode network, in particular, is activated when one's mind is at rest, when not focusing on the outside world. It has been found to improve memory, self-awareness, and for setting a true aim in life, becoming more caring to friends and family. The meditator's brain waves and structures. And we can measure these frequencies. Meditators have higher levels of alpha waves, which has been shown to reduce feelings of negative mood, tension, sadness, and anger. It also physically changes our brain's shape and size. Studies show that meditators have denser gray matter in areas associated with learning, memory processing, and emotion regulation. Yet the amygdala that deals with stress, blood pressure, and fear has decreased gray matter. We see a decrease in blood pressure and increase in the variability of heart rate. While this may sound harmful, it actually helps in in placing oxygen and carbon dioxide throughout your body. The meditators have good immune system due to meditation. If we go deeper, we can see changes in the cellular level. Your chromosomes have protective protein complexes called telomeres, which help in reducing damage to DNA and lowering cell death. And shortened telomere length has been linked to several diseases such as cardiovascular disease, diabetes, Alzheimer's, and cancer. Amazingly, when cancer survivors completed the meditation program, their bodies showed significant increase in telomere length. It's believed that the psychological intervention is particularly designed to decrease stress and has direct effects on the enzyme telomeres, which has being shown to counteract shortening by adding DNA to shrinking telomeres. Of course, meditation is not a substitute for other medical advice or healthy lifestyle. It's a way of building brain muscle. It's just like hitting the gym. It can grow your muscles and increase overall health. It seems that meditation may be a way for working out your brain. So relax and meditate.

Art is the most powerful tool in design, enhancing visual intelligence.

Michelangelo said, "A man paints with his brains and not with his hands" and "I saw the angel in the marble and carved until I set him free."

Pablo Picasso said, "Art washes away from the soul the dust of everyday life."

Art is the most powerful tool in designing and enhancing visual intelligence. Your ability to visualize and remember images, details, and awareness to the surroundings. Art sharpens your perception. Visual intelligence not only helps to form systems and work in a particular system but also works on parallel aspects of thinking out of the box. Art and science goes hand in hand. Art is the basic tool for performing major surgeries. Art is the tool in designing the bigger concepts in any field. Even the structures that are formed in math and physics are basically art related. Languages have their own artistic touch.

Art is a diverse range of human activities in creating visual, auditor, or performing artifacts and artworks expressing the creator's imaginations and technical skill, intended to be appreciated for their beauty or emotional power. In their most general form, these activities include the production of works of art, the criticism of art, the study of the history of art, and the aesthetic dissemination of art.

The oldest documented forms of art are visual arts, which include creation of images or objects in fields (including today), painting, sculpture, printmaking, photography, and other visual media.

Architecture is often included as one of the visual arts; however, like the decorative art, or advertising, it involves the creation of objects where the practical considerations of use are essential in a way that they usually are not in a painting, for example. Music, theater, film, dance, and other performances, as well as literature and other media such as interactive media, are included in a broader definition of art or the art.

Until the seventeenth century, art referred to any skill or mastery and was not differentiated from crafts or sciences.

In modern usage, after the seventeenth century, where aesthetic considerations are paramount, the fine arts are separated and distinguished from acquired skills in general, such as the decorative or applied art.

Art may be characterized in terms of mimesis, its representation of reality, narrative (storytelling), expression, communication of emotion, or other qualities. During the Romantic period, art came to be seen as "a special faculty of the human mind to be classified with religion and science."

Though the definition of what constitutes art is disputed and has changed over time, general descriptions mention an idea of imaginative or technical skill stemming from human agency of creation.

The nature of art and related concepts, such as creativity and interpretation, are explored in a branch of philosophy called aesthetic.

Forces around us attract what we think. If we think negatively, the negative dimensional field is created, and if we think positively, that positive dimensional field is created. The more we think, the more it multiplies. Sometimes we need to think negatively. It's not that we have to be positive all the time about the approach. It depends on the circumstances. Like for grief, you have to be negative to mourn or grieve over someone, but if it is with a positive approach, it's like it adds up positively, like - + + - - + + - - + + +. So it keeps adding to the thoughts, the energy produced by the brain. These energies are in the form of all chemicals in the body and mind.

So it's good to think that whatever is from the heart, the brain transmits to the heart the sensory sign. You know deep within what is right, and you should follow that and the signs that the brain sends to the heart, and the − sends to the heart creates an energy field, the chakras of the body and mind. So it's always right to say the old saying "Do good and good will happen to you." We create our own karmas by our own thinking. Therefore, we have approached our training program as networking.

Meditation

What is meditation? Every second we are meditating, our breath is doing that. It is something that you connect to something that you do work or play name it. Focus your mind. The deeper you focus, the deeper you are in meditative state. It can be anything you can connect to. The deeper you connect to the meditated state, the more pleasures you receive and the more desires are fulfilled. Doing the play or work, it becomes very pleasurable, and you feel in the moment of completeness. However, it's not easy to connect with something or anything. It's not easy to unite. Everyone has different capacities to connect; however, anyone can extend the bandwidth and balance the connection. But keeping in mind and fixating the mind, you can connect with anything you want.

Relaxing the mind is also a meditative state of mind. As we relax the central core, that's the complete absorption (samadhi in yoga). Meditation will the energy in you, and you feel healthier and happier if you connect to positive ions; however, you can also connect negatively, which takes you in a dark world that's not centrally focused. So keep in mind the "do, do, do" game. Thinking too much on various issues and not concentrating or having rigid thoughts leads to a dark world. Think less and work more or play the story of your life. It will lead to immense happiness. It's like taking a bath in eternal water in a loop connecting to a source that's centrally focused. Indulge in inward thinking. Prayer is a very powerful tool of meditation. Do pray; it's like cleaning up your mind box and keeping your ideas clear to someone supreme above as a central force.

Do you think

Competitiveness

Vying

Creates jealousy?

Love today is locking then blocking then unblocking to unlocking

and blocking.

Quite

Yet

No

Abuse

Audacity

Fashions the world.

Grit is global.

Perfection

Needs

Affection

Very

Truly

Yours

Universe

World systems will unite and be robotized

In the mere future

To keep humanity up.

What should be done?

Playing or working skillfully with action is the whole point rather than doodling.

Awareness in action.

Tricks of manipulation can be caught in unscrupulous ways of art or ingenuity.

Cast creep chase

However

Future is unknown

Embellishment

Is

Fulfillment.

Hence, take pride.

Safety feature

Hearts have no boarder lines

Need land to ground

Need air and water pumps

Hilarious as hearts are split

Funny!

Ball in my court.

Ball in your court.

Ball is bouncing to be out of court.

Color and tint reflect the consciousness.

Mind is an aura or energy field

That

Connects

To the tenth dimension.

The more you know yourself, the more mystical, magical you are

To the world.

That's the truth of a psychic

Secret.

Demarcation

Of locations

Need

A merger that's humane,

The mind is the only tool that can create it.

LOL.

Algorithm of a queen bee is like an

ENTJ personality—

Very committed to honey.

Condemn

Someone to

Extend the bandwidth of the mind. Don't demoralize anyone; you can be in Cinderella's shoes.

Healers healing

Mentors acknowledging

Psychic readings

Are beliefs actually angled on an axis of an imaginary line created by thinking?

So heal yourself. The world is the best place to live in.

Let go

Here we go

Deflate

Doesn't mean to give up, but stand up for tomorrow as it never dies.

Love is kind.

The Almighty made it.

So as we stay humble

Thinking of desires, full of expectations are very deadly abuse. Love all.

Rollicking luck is abbreviated by doing nothing in a pressured moment

Barely barring action.

Rational stocks are a superlative thought.

Purple and rainbow

Colors

Give a sense of

Unity in custody

Index exponentially roots minimize the calibration constant to the velocity, for all initial conditions of the radius (r) and velocity (v) then the azimuthal acceleration (aφ) is always zero to the central force to make a statement.

Belle

Vision

Invincibility

Obviously obligated

Diamond—

Flawless, basic, transparent, frequently and beautifully compelling, rapidly gleaming

Timidly keen, and deafeningly wealthy but excruciatingly archaic.

"Like me. Follow me."

It increases the dopamine and serotonin in my brain's chemistry, physically leading toward fitness foals that sculptures antiquity, adapting to the genetically modified to eat carefully, and performing emendation in reverse order of protection. I don't know how much time you have in understanding and acting the motion.

Nil adrift dissipates if you glaze for it.

Artistry

Not creative

Without venture

Belief in design and restraining impulsiveness can engineer prospects that are probable.

I pray.

Hoaxer hoaxes no one

Clappin' magician pranks, clappin' so hard

Psychic jest clappin' extra hard

Why do you do that?

You think he gotcha, but what you need to gotcha is hoax

To be blindfolded is to block your senses to lead without spectrum in the universe of dark energy taking off to empower.

Concealing to endeavor is for a compromise with a consented agreement on judgment; hence, make no acumen.

Prayers

Are a

True reflection of your soul.

Equation of quotation is leashed to the administer doers who are trusted on demand.

We need

Relationships to connect

And cogitate to triumph.

Jeopardy

Is

Zero.

In case you know, a nil and clumsy thing is a man who knows nothing about tomorrow, so have fun in the moment.

You can find yourself on Google too. Everything can only be on Google if you are there.

You need a touch full of multiple relationships. Just the support does work, but DNA does like the touch. Mother Nature, too, harnesses the same touch. Don't leave anyone alone or lonely. Help, serve, sacrifice, protect, and care.

The mind

Can convex

The concave molecules into dimensions beyond existence.

The more we fancy,

The more paradox are

Fabricated.

We all lie. Truth is wanted by all, but truth is difficult to grasp in complexity. By simply taking sat nam, you achieve it.

I am

That fragrance

I am

When I came across you, you told me who I am in duality

Beauty of

Beauty keeps changing formats like a mutant, yet beauty is incongruity of thoughts.

Music

Is an antidote to pain.

Play in harmony.

The new unconscious

The sublime

Previews and perceive things fancier and embellished, yet the things are the same

Be active

Not

Proactive

Don't try to overcontrol others and yourself.

The power of get-together is so much that it purifies your soul and coagulates connections.

So connect to dine.

I have no prank

However

Crisis crave you new opportunities to shell out new ways into the subsequent.

Spark to ignite.

Enlightening your soul is an art, not magic.

Sometimes you are not overwhelmed.

You are crushed, you need empathy.

A good thought or a good deed is done for today, and yes, you will soon be OK. 😊

The person who can read love in your eyes is a true master of all and jack of none—no one but God.

You make schedules.

You make regimes.

But unless you don't train your brain, you haven't done anything. Install to autopilot

The person who can read love in your eyes is a true master of all and jack of none—no one but God.

Dil se

De memoria

Par Coeur

I am one; that's the truth.

I almost fling in catastrophe

That your love was handmade for me when it's just a war of powers.

Quitting

Is suicidal.

You quit and stumble, you are losing your chances forever, and Gabrielle can't help. Just do the necessary. Be a player.

Be cognizant of the political boundaries within which you work.

We are people. We all live in it.

Phobia—

What will people think, say?

They are gonna laugh at me.

If I use simple words, you will not know the significance of what I fabricate

I am

Derma is superficial. Races are hellacious. Love is vivacious, which flows in the veins, yet minds are heroic ousters.

As a child, I was a tomboy who used to daunt.

As a girl, I was a pretty sob who used to haunt.

As woman getting much matured, cosmopolitan, enlightened, and passionate, I was learning new ways for daunting prospects, still searching curiously.

Action and happiness are deeply connected.

Happiness is action, and friendship the key.

The more superior systems of operation we have in the league, the better is the camouflage for enforcement of law and order.

You can never speck luck

It

Twinkles

Arbitrarily

This is what I want

This is what I don't want.

This is what it looks like.

I am chaffing

Designed proposal

Not so primitive

Yet digital

Resilient people are not getting better or worse than

Flexible

Creating new horizons is all idiosyncratic

Saying

Forgive and forget

No one forgives and forgets

Memory comes and goes

Ego is bigger than your heart

Days, weeks, months, years shall travel

In time

We will live and die for love♡

In love we trust

The

Code of conduct

Articulates

The deportment; it's the way you say it

We all love beauty.

Beauty is made of plastic that's cynical and sarcastic and keeps changing formats.

We should not love beauty. See the beauty side for attachments, as they will last longer.

"In love we trust" should not be based only on beauty.

You don't have to fidget.

God automatically gives you what's paramount.

Go with the flow.

We know that we have to jump out, and still, we don't jump out.

Either we are powerless or inflexible or both.

Jump out, guys. We need to jump out.

Devour

Devotion

Endearment

Is all we aspire for

When the finite

Tries to match the infinite in mindfulness, they become one

It's the awakening of your immortality

I am

Being solicitous to your kids is your motive; I believe it makes

Intimate

Association

Patios that melt in your brain are the dialects of grace and are the

Languages of love

Seeing artifacts in a flawless mode is closely packed than seeing them in complexity.

Altruistic

Humanitarian

Philanthropic

You are able to be

Are you that gem?

Field land of lucid dreams in immortality

Reaching the source of the universe, searching for harmony is contemplation

Love is the language where equality doesn't filter.

Love maximum.

Dream on Loyalty

I had a dream. I was a warrior, a patrician, a chief of the battalion, a strong, bold, and masculine person who can make decisions on the move, moving swiftly. I was a chief to the imperial blood, a beautiful princess👑. I was trying to protect her from the shooting of the opposite of the army, which happened on sudden grounds. I acted with supernatural zeal and ability and very primitive-style-oriented. Highly trained, I cut through and passed. I aimed the shot right in the heads of the soldier. I struck them, those who are the antagonists in my whole lucid dream. At the end, the assassination was mine. I hence took a bullet to save that beautiful daughter of the monarch who was so scared and timid to take any action. She was confused. She needed to be safeguarded. I had been ordered to shield her. I did my duty right and slaughtered my life for her, and she must have always thought that I was a person of noble blood (altruistic). She was entitled to royalty👑. I was no royal, but loyal. I suddenly felt unusually emotional. I had qualms. Why did I have that dream?

If you are arrogant

You

Collapse, and it's your

Pitfall

Yoga isn't only a gymnastics

It's a program

For the body and mind

Hence, it isn't only for youth yoga

Holistic discipline

Harmonizing the body, mind and spirit

Yoga citta vritti nirodhah

Keep memories

In a photograph

Store them in the clouds

When memories hit you

Most importantly, keep them in your heart and mind

Time factor only matters

While we are alive

We have life, we are in the time zone

What stays behind are the memories

The union

Is

Yoga

Unites everybody from anywhere in

Serenity

Empower women to come out of financial crises

What are we doing?

My question is, What are the citizens doing for equality?

Socially, everyone is treated equal

Not only under law and order

The blindfold on Themis suggests justice is blind. She has foresight, knowing the secret unknown as a protector of the oppressed and a protector of hospitality.

The blindfold holds symbolism that has roots in antiquity, arguably archetypes of culture itself. Those depicted as having great insight or intuition are traditionally depicted as blinded in some way. This gives one the power to see reality through the symbolic "third eye" which penetrates the facades or illusions of life allowing one to see the truth.

Delete or hide this

Love is

Caring, sharing

Mind matching. No two fingers are equal, still connected to the hand. Love is unity and strength.

Does love construct a perfect outcome, like a happy ending of a fairy tale, or is it a psychological disorder of immensity?

Smile and the world smiles with you.

Reflections of the man

Show in his dignity

And the woman in her attitude

Patience is tolerating delay. It's not suffering. It's to act without a tornado of rage silently killing with soft songs.

Before the rivalry begins

The clause "To keep or not keep"

Insult or let go

It's a one-take show

On the screen of life, reinsurance not guaranteed

Kill egos, not hearts♡

Heal the heart

Your undesirable product is your fault. Create your own markets and refine.

Everything can go to waste if not utilized

Well.

Roast your food well.

There is definitely good and bad.

You distinguish between fragrance, fulfillment, and shit. Shit needs to be let out.

Don't hump back on naysayers

Excel with a "Yes, it's possible."

Honestly, don't live in self-denial.

If it's a snake, it's a snake. If it's a rope, it's a rope. Matter and materials differ.

That's different. You are so strong. You aren't bothered of a rope being a snake. For you, they are irrelevant. It will only happen with a strong core and inner strength. You don't fear, you overcome your fears. First comes acceptance to the reality, knowing the difference, not acting ignorant. But living in self-denial is stupidity.

When being a musician, you want an audience, not critics and go-getters

You want a listening heart ♡

I play, you listen 👂 *attitude*

I am here. I never left.

I am in the game. Call me if you need me.

Like to learn with mutual understanding,

With mutual understanding,

Respecting friends with mutual consent, loving the knowledge, respecting for knowledge, but still keeping you at equality with my own self. No one is high or low.

Everyone should respect ✊ one another equally.

Drawing the pictures in different sizes, hoping it's making a difference to someone somewhere to prosper and enhance. Thank you.

Having life and being alive are the most important parts about you

You can change all your actions

Time reveals

Everyone has to face their own 😼 demons.

Learn that if being straight doesn't help get the work done, use reverse psychology in a positive way.

Interdependency is important and caring. If someone can depend on you for something, you aren't a soul sucker. If they can't depend on you, it's your fault. You have to take actions into play, do something productive for them to depend on you, and if they still can't depend on you, you need to make decisions and changes in the social and environmental patterns. It's hard and tiring to explain in a simple way.

You can't build elephants by putting your own weight on them 'cause you, too, are the same species. You can't put your whole load on just one person. You can't put your whole load on just one person. You have to show interdependency. If you don't, there will be turbulence, and you will fall down. So does the whole race. Unity is strength. It's always good to bring something to the table. Don't act dumb. When you do, not everyone has something else to contribute. Put your contribution and make others realize what you get to the table in a way they understand, not like a baby 👶 who can't talk in a way others don't understand. You have to put your foot down and firm. No one is a bloodsucker. If you are, you are for a reason, but you do contribute. Show your contributions; show the design, the pattern of what you are getting; and show what benefits the others. If we do that, there will be no fights. Caring and sharing.

Go Dutch

Don't let just one person pay 💰

Don't be a parasite

It's uncomfortable

My power being a woman is, I like perfumes over

Guns and roses.

It's not nonviolence; it's just to be empowered to come out of self-denial.

Your worst enemy is the fear in self-denial.

It's like you always imagine before you create. Draw beautifully.

It's not like I see the science. I know the art; it's forever.

I see the art. I see the experiment. I did think logically. I know the science.

Art, pictures, and plays give me fine details.

I learn my majors just by observation

For me, it never ends.

I love to see.

There is only one sin, and that's the destruction to the soul by pushing it down with negative criticism.

My gratitude, my acknowledgement

Thank you for being my friend

My support and encouragement

I need friends

Not wanting to be a leader, I want to be led by my friends

I need to learn something from

Everyone—my philosophy

You will always feel like a zero if you live in stagnant waters. Find your energies, open your mind, jump.

Else, burn yourself to be a zero.

Find a purpose.

I truly believe in astro sciences. However, not all scientists create medicines; some create bombs. So be careful.

And be mindful. Either you want pollution or you want growth. It's the same with the creator too. There are things that are too good for humans to do and some we can't accept, as it will ruin us. So create energy that heals, not destroy the planet. It's my message. Money is secondary; what comes first is the life and expectancy of the creatures living on the planet. It's not like you give cancer and its cures. No, it's not acceptable.

Hope every day is a new day with a good thought 💬 *and actions to play.*

Someone told me when I was a kid

Flush the negative feelings down the toilet

You will feel good taking the waste out

Let go

Everyone has a purpose; find yours.

It's your need.

In your heart, you know it well.

No one will get depressed or sad if they get their needs fulfilled. Needs are like medicines.

You can't starve on needs or make someone starve on needs too. It's karma.

Keep your mind full.

Don't starve. Get food for the soul in a way that's healthy and nutritious for your spirit.

Best way if you lose motivation

Be friends with people who are self-motivated in action

This way, you never fall

We are the pilot of our own flight. We crash it or take and land it safely. It's up to us. We can do it with love. ♡

True listening is setting aside your own self.

Everything can be channeled if we discipline without giving harsh punishments to ourselves but utter discipline only with love.

To be happy to be single:

Learn from others as us, not me as an individual.

Learn from the groups you connect. Not even trees can stay single. They need connections. They grow in togetherness of their like minds or actions. Learning in togetherness should be like trees growing together, not like a warfare.

To my understanding in today's world, we learn from one another. We are all gurus of our choices. It's a democratic world under one satellite.

Don't try to

Overestimate things

Remember that you aren't

God

Friends with benefits are great 👍

However, there are boundaries that are not okay to break.

It's okay if they are friends only.

Set your boundaries if you see red flags ⚑ *. Good for you as it can cost a lifetime if this is missed out.*

Real powerful people

Never abuse you; they only abuse being powerless or being a victim

Effortless love ♡ *just go with the flow. It's not unconditional or conditional. It's just effortlessly loving someone.*

Value Humans

Forgiveness involves the overcoming of anger and resentment and mercy involves the withholding of harsh treatment that one has a right to inflict… There are similar paradoxes associated with mercy, particularly in the context of punishment; too strong an emphasis on mercy can lead to a departure from justice. Mercy is more than forgiveness.

Hope is a door that never closes its

Gates

Patience is tolerating delay

It's not a suffering; it's to act

Without a tornado of rage

Silently killing with the soft songs

It's a one-take show

On the real screen of life, reinsurance card not guaranteed

Before the rivalry begins

The clause

"To keep or not keep"

Insult or let go

A journey should be a happiness project. It's said that the tree which bends has the maximum fruits. Learn to bend and put a smile ☒ on yourself and others. Comedy is the hardest thing to do. But happiness projects can be achieved by smiles.

The creator will give you what you want and need if you are self-determined and consequences you have to face… Be prepared with the plan to face consequences; honestly, it's very true. That's what I learned the hard way.

Everyone deserves chances; it's yours to grab. Go around, and you will find love ♡

Don't imprison yourself. Love is all around us.

Honestly, I never plan my course.

I think very spontaneously, and I end up thinking the best course. This is very true to me. It's not that I brain dump. It's what I think. My writings are the practical experiences I have around me; so are my motivation and my community that I wish to make. I believe sometimes I act too spontaneously that I feel I type words faster than computers. That I am too connected to this reality is so true. It's me in it, and it's not a "fake it till I make it" experience. It's all what I am inside out. I love my consciousness to be at this level. I achieve what I feel righteously and rightfully by being proactive, having courage to run my mouth the power to speak through text, saying what I feel are my beliefs, and letting go of the past and be legitimately there. Hope I create harmonic wealth and well-being for the self and others.

Consciousness is neither dead nor alive. It's a free state. It's like one in a consciousness state can change their brain algorithms. They know all the logs, but they choose to remain in the stillness of life no more, no less. Consciousness is like the number 9 in string theory being the highest number, like a cloud ☁. It's like the state of being becomes a magnetic crystal personality. They have high dynamics of static consciousness; they are fulfilled. I honestly can imagine someone in this state of being able to manifest and proclaim the happiness of thought and action. It's called samadhi.

It's the highest state of consciousness. You go thoughtless, and then you rain 🍄 from the cloud ☁. If you are conscious, you connect with your own self and others without denial.

Kill egos, not hearts.

Heal the heart ♡.

Be a healer.

Your undesirable product is your fault. Create your own markets and refine.

For me, money is one of the basic needs, and I admit that without it, I can't do anything for myself or for others whom I wish to do things, either materialistic or even nonmaterialistic. Money ⑤ is very important, but getting arrogant with the power of money is not.

I write so much. I am a sage. I am mystical too. I am as good as a scientist or a so-called mystic, but not on TV, not earning anything with what I do. I spread my knowledge, my imagination for free, and free things are ignored even if they are worth adopting. Yes, people take you for granted. They think you are crazy 😵. You keep writing or being a sage, but if you do the things on TV or the media, you are getting fame and you are getting power. You are misusing people. They're innocent. It's not right; it's not fair.

A real superhorse will never show or reveal his or her identity for fame or money. If he has one dollar of his own, he will donate the seventy-five cents to the people whom he feels need it more and keep the twenty-five cents for his resources. He will be giving more than taking, not like the fake gurus or so-called matas in India. He or she will actually do things like God's plans—not only singing God's plans, making videos etc., or collecting fame but also spreading what they have for real. And for it, they are ready to face whatever it takes.

That's what Buddha says to me always. I know it may be strange, as strange as it is to me, yes. I know what I say for real 😣. I think divine powers love the sweets, the cakes, and the money you give in the temples, mosques, gurdwaras, churches, and other religious places. Is one dollar used? Even my Buddha asks this question, I feel it's a no-no. So yes, money is important. If God likes sweet so much, so do we. We like sweet. We give less and ask more—no, it should be give more, give more, give more and more.

In duality, we exist only if we let go of the darkness. Nights shall pass to the brightest days. Forget about winning or losing; just play. In duality, we exist only if we let go of the darkness. Nights shall pass to the brightest days. Forget about winning or losing; just play.

www.ingramcontent.com/pod-product-compliance
Lightning Source LLC
Chambersburg PA
CBHW071107120626
46546CB00003B/1292